Junk Drawer

poems by

Corey D. Cook

Finishing Line Press
Georgetown, Kentucky

Junk Drawer

Copyright © 2022 by Corey D. Cook
ISBN 978-1-64662-723-3 First Edition
All rights reserved under International and Pan-American Copyright Conventions. No part of this book may be reproduced in any manner whatsoever without written permission from the publisher, except in the case of brief quotations embodied in critical articles and reviews.

ACKNOWLEDGMENTS

Grateful acknowledgment is made to the editors of the following publications in which these pieces first appeared (some in earlier versions and some under different titles).

Self-Interview: *Ibbetson Street*
A Note to Donald Hall: *Northern New England Review*
the army captain at home or a father helping with chores: *Dead Snakes*
under the chuppah…: *Brevities*
Depressed and Driving to Work in February (Looking for Something to Sustain Me): *Silent Auctions Magazine*
Early springtime: *the Aurorean*
Donald Hall Estate Sale: *Freshwater*
Lake Morey: *Plum Tree Tavern*
Shucking Corn: *Red River Review*
making dinner…: *Poem Town—Bradford, VT*
still not speaking…: *Akitsu Quarterly*
Fishing: *Boston Literary Magazine*
Country Song: *Poppy Road Review*
Splitting Wedge: *Trouvaille Review*
Dead Cow on Route 5 During the Pandemic: *Ink Pantry*
fatherless boy…: *Brevities*
Sitting in the Yard After My Vasectomy: *Silent Auctions Magazine*
At the Donald Hall and Jane Kenyon Estate Sale: *Smoky Quartz*
Adrift: *The Mountain Troubadour*
mourning dove provides…: *Brevities*
Sitting in the Paved Driveway: *The Mountain Troubadour*
"Writing" Poems with Three Children: *Ariel Chart*
Meeting the Poet David Budbill in a Dream: *Muddy River Poetry Review*
metal tacklebox…: *Poem Town—Bradford, VT*
Commuting to Work in Early March After a Breakthrough in Therapy: *Viscaria Review*

Publisher: Leah Huete de Maines
Editor: Christen Kincaid
Cover Art: Cristina Clarimon
Author Photo: Rachael D. Cook
Cover Design: Elizabeth Maines McCleavy

Order online: www.finishinglinepress.com
also available on amazon.com

Author inquiries and mail orders:
Finishing Line Press
PO Box 1626
Georgetown, Kentucky 40324
USA

Table of Contents

Self-Interview 1
A Note to Donald Hall 3
the army captain at home or a father helping with chores 4
Junk Drawer (I) 5
under the chuppah 5
Depressed and Driving to Work in February (Looking for
    Something to Sustain Me) 6
Early springtime 7
Donald Hall Estate Sale 8
Junk Drawer (II) 10
Lake Morey 11
Shucking Corn 12
making dinner 13
Junk Drawer (III) 14
still not speaking 15
Fishing 16
Country Song 17
Splitting Wedge 18
Junk Drawer (IV) 19
Dead Cow on Route 5 During the Pandemic 20
fatherless boy 21
Sitting in the Yard After My Vasectomy 22
At the Donald Hall and Jane Kenyon Estate Sale 23
Adrift 24
mourning dove provides 25
Sitting in the Paved Driveway 26
Junk Drawer (V) 28
"Writing" Poems with Three Children 29
Meeting the Poet David Budbill in a Dream 30
metal tacklebox 32
Commuting to Work in Early March After a Breakthrough
    in Therapy 33

For Rachael

*In memory of Kevin M. Harvey (1948-2020)
& Cindy Kelly Benabderrahman (1977-2021)*

Self-Interview

How do you feel?

Like Sisyphus
working against

the immense weight
of his boulder—

shackled,
and wearing

a lead vest.

What is your state of mind?

My mind is a papery wasp nest.
Thoughts white larvae—

present, but dormant
and malleable.

Lacking the wings
which would enable them

to take flight.

> "...you lay down
> on top of me, pressing
> the bile of desolation into every pore..."

—*Having it Out with Melancholy* by Jane Kenyon

> "...This thing between us, has wings, it has teeth
> It has got horns and feathers, and sinews beneath..."

—*Jacob and the Angel* by Suzanne Vega

A Note to Donald Hall

I have cautiously crawled past your house.
Slithered around the damp edge of Eagle Pond.

Peered up canopied New Canada Road.
I wasn't stalking you,

but the land that inspires you.
My limbs and head

remained in my shell of silver-blue metal.
Your words…stood on the porch

and raised shotguns.
Your words…POSTED signs

nailed to the trees on the bank of Eagle Pond.
Your words…piles of scat

on the shoulder of New Canada Road.
I was trespassing.

The exhaust pipe tucked between the two back tires
and the car retreated.

the army captain at home or a father helping with chores

screen door slams

seconds later
he rounds
the corner
of the house

laundry basket
lodged under
his left arm

steam rising
from cloth diapers

he approaches
the line

clothespins
stand at attention

Junk Drawer (I)

Box of pushpins
purchased years before
in a bustling
college bookstore.

Photocopied marriage certificate,
our jittery signatures
side by side.

Green-handled awl
you inherited
from your grandmother.

Scribbled on a cocktail napkin:

>*under the chuppah*
>*two shadows*
>*become one*

Single bag of popcorn
that will gestate
in the microwave
in two to four minutes.

**Depressed and Driving to Work in February
(Looking for Something to Sustain Me)**

a figure by the side
of the road,
last week's snowman,
winnowed down,
brined with sand,
with salt,
spindly arm raised
in a tenuous wave

Early springtime

and each new leaf
on the bush
outside my window
is more perfect
than the next,

diminutive
and round,
unblemished
and burgeoning,

like our daughter's toes
at the water's edge.

Donald Hall Estate Sale
for my parents

The line formed
in front of the long face
of the barn.

Under a latticework
of tree limbs,
limbs etched into sky,
into memory,
limbs giving way
to slight leaves,
noncommittal on a cold,
cloud-filled morning.

Formed to the left
of the ox cart,
clumps of manure still waiting
to be shoveled,
spread in the field…

Inside the bookshelves sagged
under the weight of his work,
my fingers stuttered
over their spines
until I reached the stairs
to the second floor,
the stairs with the orange shag carpet,
the carpet punctuated
with mouse droppings,
remnants of unrelenting revision,
commas and hyphens and periods
that anchored what once was,
what was unneeded,
like the hot air rising
from the registers in the floor,

despite all the bustling bodies,
red-faced as they moved
from room to room,
picking things up,
putting things down,
bagging what they intended
to take away.

I just wanted him back
at his desk,
pad of paper ready,
pen in hand.

Just wanted Jane upstairs
in her office,
glasses in place,
fingers poised
above the typewriter's keys.

So I let myself out,
stepped off the porch,
followed the line
to its unceremonious end.

Junk Drawer (II)

Stripped pencil,
eraser gnawed off.

Used candles,
back in the packaging,
stubby,
wicks stiff
and black.

H's metallic-blue barrette,
holding fast
to a single strand
of hair,
a lucid
and delicate lifeline.

Old passwords
on an index card.

To-do list,
not one item
crossed off.

Two-dollar bill,
heavily creased
and starting to tear.

Lake Morey

Red and white bobber pins the sky's
reflection to the surface of the lake,
an expanse of light blue borrowed
from Picasso, crowded with schools
of clouds, their bellies round and ripe.

Shucking Corn

Nana sits at the kitchen table shucking corn.
Her leathery face sprouting from faded overalls.
Intently watches her favorite soap on the portable tv
as she drops husks into a metal bowl between her feet.

Husks I soon bring to the pigs in the back yard.
Their flat snouts lined up over the long trough.

When I walk back into the house
a male star has been stripped of his shirt.
His heaving chest is chiseled and glistening.
Nana stares at the screen and her mouth hangs open.

Moments later she clears her throat and announces:
I'd gladly scrub my clothes on that washboard.

making dinner...

making dinner
after couples counseling
pot boils over

Junk Drawer (III)

Dried-up yellow highlighter.

Slim brown button
that once adorned
the low-cut blouse
you ripped up,
turned into cleaning rags.

E's quickly rendered artwork,
a series of short squiggles
entitled *snakes*,
no venom-laced fangs,
no forked tongues,
just supple bodies.

Grey seashell,
gleaned from a honey-
moon beach,
gritty sand
still inside.

Dozens of outlet covers,
ready to block
a toddler's
prodding fingers.

Expired fishing license,
folded in half
like a closed book.

Local phone directory,
just released,
Nana's number
no longer listed.

still not speaking…

still not speaking
you hang diapers on the line
so many white flags

Fishing
> *for my father (June 16, 2019)*

He must be
a hundred miles away,
trolling for lake trout
on Champlain.

I can picture
his freckled shoulders,
the tacklebox
with its rusty latch,
the lures,
their barbed hooks
like inverted talons,
dangling two by two,
the downriggers
that will take
the lifeless decoys
and drag them towards
the rocky bottom.

I can picture
the open mouth
of the net,
its handle
just within reach.

Country Song

Blue bicycle leans against the sagging
barn. As the strawflower's stiff petals

pluck at its spokes. And the Mourning
Dove's solitary song rises with the sun.

Splitting Wedge

-Yesterday-

We found it in the garage,
on a grease-stained shelf,
tap-tap-tapped it into place,
raised the sledgehammer
above the obstinate log—
gnarled hardwood—
and delivered seven blows.

It sank deeper and deeper
until the halves fell away.

-Last Night-

We slept back to back
until our youngest tiptoed in,
lodged himself between us.

He slept fitfully,
thrashed and shuttered,
his toenails sharp,
head hard and punishing.

He woke early and slipped out
of bed for Sesame Street
and the letter of the day,
leaving behind the "V" our bodies made,
our heels barely touching.

Junk Drawer (IV)

Headless dinosaur
lying on its side
in the lid
of a canning jar.

Clipped and forgotten coupons,
unused gift certificates.

My counselor's business card,
the suicide prevention
phone number
hastily written
on the back,
just in case.

O's report card
from swim lessons,
the one skill unchecked:
survival float.

Dead Cow on Route 5 During the Pandemic

It had been dragged to the edge of the field,
now just a mound inside the barbed wire

fence, the windowed panel of a wedding tent
draped over it, failing to hide the mottled coat,

bloated body, as I drive by in the northbound lane,
following the saturated bank of the Connecticut

River, thinking of those whose lungs have become
wet sponges, who are slowly drowning, dying alone.

fatherless boy...

fatherless boy
runs his fingers
over my stubble

Sitting in the Yard after My Vasectomy

        in and)
                (out of
the crumbling)
                (stone wall
    the loose)
                (sutures of
  a snake)

At the Donald Hall and Jane Kenyon Estate Sale

Others were there for the antiques,
baseball memorabilia.

I returned again and again to their books,
titles and covers as familiar as old friends.

Found three inscribed by Jane,
her signature drawn-out and fluid in the first two,
deliberate and jagged in the third,
as if brought to her as she sat in bed,
propped up by pillows,
pen unwieldy in her waning hand,
on one of those last days.

Adrift

Somehow my mother becomes
a sailboat the night
my grandmother dies.

She rocks at the bedside
until the final breath
comes,
goes.

The final breath
that propels her forward.

Causes her to drift
out of the room,
aimless and unseaworthy,
into the open arms
of family members,
offering their temporary coves.

But she is inconsolable,
restless,
sets out again.

Makes it to the mudroom,
where a man sits smoking
by an open window,
the tip of his cigarette
a lantern,
guiding her ashore
as he stands,
steadfast as a mooring bollard,
her husband,
my father.

mourning dove provides…

mourning dove provides
soundtrack for pallbearers'
slow procession

Sitting in the Paved Driveway

The white towels hang heavy
and straight on the clothesline.

We sit meters apart,
in aluminum folding chairs,
avoiding eye contact,
wringing our hands.

As E feeds dandelion greens
to the chickens,
their curved beaks
clamping down,
ripping,
reducing each jagged leaf
to a thready stump.

As O studies the car's grille,
a man-made web,
its gruesome contents,
runs her forefinger
and thumb down
the impossibly thin wing
of a dragonfly.

As H crouches down
with a box of chalk,
starts drawing narrow roads
and lopsided buildings.

Buildings soon upstaged
by a red-leafed bush
trembling in one corner
of the yard.
Out of desperation?
Anger?

As the blank face
of the sunflower
looks on,
reminiscent of our counselor's face
just hours before,
embarrassed,
unsure of what to say,
what to suggest.

I lean forward and stare
at the ground,
surprised to see
that I am now sitting
in the middle
of an intersection,
a tricycle and two bikes
lined up behind me,
my wife standing off
to the side,
her arms crossed,
all four staring,
all four waiting
for me
to do something.

Junk Drawer (V)

Roll of Kodak film,
never developed,
faces of loved ones
coiled inside,
the tightest embrace.

Pennies in a plastic bag.

Hydration solution ingredients
neatly printed
on a scrap
of yellow construction paper,
the solution our kids
chocked down,
refused to drink again
after the latest bug…

> *6 tablespoons of sugar*
> *½ teaspoon of salt*
> *1 liter of water*

Valid fishing license,
lucky lures listed
on the back.

His and hers phone chargers
in an inexplicable knot,
bound together
like a solemn vow.

"Writing" Poems with Three Children

Means repeating the words over
and over in your head, hoping

to commit them, or at least some,
to memory, as you pick up socks shed

at the door, pick up abandoned art,
crumb-covered plates, the overturned

basket of balls, as you wash, fold,
and put away another load of laundry,

pack dairy-free and nut-free lunches,
as you watch your son string cars together

on the stairs, line after enviable line.

Meeting the Poet David Budbill in a Dream

I was surprised
to see the self-proclaimed
recluse on a sidewalk
in Cleveland, Ohio.

Wearing Levi's
and a t-shirt.

Self-assured,
deftly maneuvering
through the crowds
he shunned
for Judevine Mountain.

I struggled to keep up,
saw him duck
into a café,
settle at the counter.

Worked up the nerve
to approach him,
introduce myself.

He shook my hand
and gestured
to the stool
next to his.

We spoke
of migrating birds
and black flies.

He asked if I would
join him for tea.

I accepted the invitation
and promptly woke up,
my bedroom curtains steeped
in early morning light,
an empty cup
on the nightstand.

metal tacklebox...

metal tacklebox
bobbers and barbed hooks
his corncob pipe

Commuting to Work in Early March after a Breakthrough in Therapy

I
snow recedes,
loosens its stranglehold,
releases parched leaves,
leaves that scuttle and scrape across blacktop

II
raven rises from a deer's ribcage,
wings beating,
feathers dark and iridescent,
feet tucked

III
stonewall encircles a field of stubble,
interlocking boulders,
weathered,
worn as ancestral rosary beads

IV
cardboard box sits in the median,
flaps open,
poised to receive impending rain,
the promise of sunlight

Corey D. Cook is the author of five previous poetry collections. His most recent, *The Weight of Shadows*, was also released by Finishing Line Press (2019). Corey has had over 270 poems published in print and online magazines since 2004. His work has appeared in *Akitsu Quarterly, As It Ought To Be, Boston Literary Magazine, Brevities, Cold Moon Journal, Freshwater, Ink Pantry, The Mountain Troubadour, Muddy River Poetry Review, Nixes Mate Review, Silent Auctions Magazine, Trouvaille Review* and *Viscaria Magazine*. Corey edited *The Orange Room Review* with his wife, Rachael, for eight years (2006-2014) and he currently edits *Red Eft Review*. He works at a hospital and lives in East Thetford, Vermont.

www.ingramcontent.com/pod-product-compliance
Lightning Source LLC
LaVergne TN
LVHW040116080426
835507LV00041B/1101